This Journal Belongs to

Published by

Workplace Wonders

Made in the USA
Middletown, DE
01 April 2025

73637677R00067